YOU, THE MISSIONARY

Committing To and Participating In God's Worldwide Mission

A Guide for Believers Who Desire to Become Missional Christians in Missional Churches

Ebbie C. Smith

Church Starting Network
2009

YOU THE MISSIONARY:
Committing to and Participating In God's Worldwide Mission

© Copyright Ebbie C. Smith
2009

All rights reserved

Library of Congress Cataloging-in-Publication Data

Ebbie C. Smith

ISBN 978-0-9825079-1-9

1. Missionary Methods   2. Title   3. Short-term Missions   3. Lay workers

Church Starting Network
3515 Sycamore School Road
Ste 125 Box 161
Ft. Worth, Texas 76133

www.ChurchStarting.net

Resources: Church Starting Network

Church Starting and Growth

English

Daniel R. Sánchez, Ebbie C. Smith, and Curtis Watke, *Starting Reproducing Congregations: A Guidebook for Contextual New Church Development.* Ft. Worth, Texas: Church Starting Network, 2001. (www.churchstarting.net)

Daniel R. Sánchez, Ebbie C. Smith, and Curtis Watke. *Starting Reproducing Congregations Strategy Planner: A Workbook for Contextual New Church Development.* Ft. Worth, Texas: Church Starting Network, 2001. (www.churchstarting.net)

Ebbie C. Smith, *Growing Healthy Churches: New Directions for Church Growth in the 21st Century.* Ft. Worth, Texas: Church Starting Network, 2003. (www.churchstarting.net)

Daniel R. Sánchez & Rudolph González. *Sharing the Good News with Our Roman Catholic Friends.* Ft. Worth, Texas: Church Starting Network, 2004. (www.churchstarting.net)

Daniel R. Sánchez, *Gospel in the Rosary.* Ft. Worth, Texas: Church Starting Network, 2004. (www.churchstarting.net)

Ebbie C. Smith. *Spiritual Warfare for 21st Century Christians.* Ft. Worth, Texas: Church Starting Network, 2005. (www.churchstarting.net)

Daniel R. Sánchez, ed., *Church Planting Movements in North America.* Ft. Worth, Texas: Church Starting Network, 2007. (www.churchstarting.net)

Daniel R. Sánchez, *Hispanic Realities Impacting America: Implications for Evangelism and Missions.* Ft. Worth, Texas: Church Starting Network, 2006. (www.churchstarting.net)

Ebbie C. Smith, *Basic Churches are Real Churches.* Ft. Worth, Texas: Church Starting Network, 2009. (www.churchstarting.net)

Spanish

Daniel R. Sánchez, Ebbie C. Smith, and Curtis Watke, *Como Sembrar Iglesias en el Siglo XXI.* El Paso, Texas: Casa Bautista de Publicaciones, 2001. *www.sembrariglesias.net* (www.churchstarting.net)

Daniel R. Sánchez, Ebbie C. Smith, and Curtis Watke, *Mis Planes Estratégicos Para Sembrar Iglesias en El Siglo XXI: Libro de trabajo para el desarrollo contextual de una iglesia nueva.* Ft. Worth, Texas: Church Starting Network, 2002. *www.sembrariglesias.net* (www.churchstarting.net)

Daniel R. Sánchez, Ebbie C. Smith, *Cultivando Iglesias Saludables.* Ft. Worth, Texas: Church Starting Network, 2008. www.sembrariglesias.net (www.churchstarting.net)

Daniel R. Sánchez, Rodolfo González. *Comparta Las Buenas Nuevas Con Sus Amigos Católicos.* Ft. Worth, Texas: Church Starting Network, 2004. www.sembrariglesias.net (www.churchstarting.net)

Daniel R. Sánchez. *Evangelio En El Rosario.* Ft. Worth, Texas: Church Starting Network, 2004. www.sembrariglesias.net (www.churchstarting.net)

Daniel R. Sánchez. *Iglesia: Crecimiento y Cultura*. Ft. Worth, Texas: Church Starting Network, 2004. www.sembrariglesias.net (www.churchstarting.net)

Daniel R. Sánchez. *Manual para Implementar Crecimiento y Cultura.* Ft. Worth, Texas: Church Starting Network, 2004. www.sembrariglesias.net (www.churchstarting.net)

Daniel R. Sánchez. *Realidades Hispanas Que Impactan A América: Implicaciones para Evangelización y Misiones.* Ft. Worth, Texas: Church Starting Network, 2006. www.sembrariglesias.net (www.churchstarting.net)

J.O. Terry, *Guía Para La Narrativa Bíblica* (Synopsis of the Bible Storying Handbook, translated into Spanish by Keith Stamps). Ft. Worth, Texas: Church Starting Network, 2008. www.sembrariglesias.net (www.churchstarting.net)

Bible Storying Resources

J.O Terry, *Basic Bible Storying.* Ft. Worth, Texas: Church Starting Network, 2006. (www.churchstarting.net)

Daniel R. Sánchez, J.O. Terry, LaNette Thompson. *Bible Storying for Church Planting.* Ft. Worth, Texas: Church Starting Network, 2008. (www.churchstarting.net)

J.O. Terry, *Bible Storying Handbook: For Short-Term Church Mission Teams and Mission Volunteers.* Ft. Worth, Texas: Church Starting Network, 2008. (www.churchstarting.net)

J.O. Terry, *Guía Para La Narrativa Bíblica* (Synopsis of the Bible Storying Handbook, translated into Spanish by Keith Stamps). Ft. Worth, Texas: Church Starting Network, 2008. (www.churchstarting.net)

J.O. Terry, *Hope Stories from the Bible.* Ft. Worth, Texas: Church Starting Network, 2008. (www.churchstarting.net)

Daniel R. Sánchez and J.O. Terry. *LifeStory Encounters.* Ft. Worth, Texas: Church Starting Network, 2009. (www.churchstarting.net)

J. O. Terry, *Death Stories from the Bible.* Ft. Worth, Texas: Church Starting Network, 2009. (www.churchstarting.net)

v

J. O. Terry, *Food Stories from the Bible.* Ft. Worth, Texas: Church Starting Network, 2009. (www.churchstarting.net)

J. O. Terry, *Grief Stories from the Bible.* Ft. Worth, Texas: Church Starting Network, 2009. (www.churchstarting.net)

The Church Starting Network supplies all of these resources:

3515 Sycamore School Road, Fort Worth, Texas 76133

www.ChurchStarting.net

www.sembrariglesias.net

Dedication

Dedicated to those Christians who, even if they do not recognize it, are missionaries. The prayer of this book is that
God's people everywhere will realize and accept
the fact and act on the truth that *they are missionaries.*

Do not look for missionaries—You are the missionary

Contents

Preface

You, if you are a believer in the Lord Jesus Christ, **are a missionary.** You may have never traveled to a distant country nor preached a sermon in the traditional way. You may have never healed a dreaded disease nor taught a Bible class. You may have never written a book nor composed a Christian song. But still, *you are a missionary.*

The essence of this book is that every Christian is a missionary and should be engaged directly in God's redemptive work in this world. The book further declares that every church should be a missional church engaged directly in God's missionary activity. This book calls for every Christian and every church to become missional in nature.

Missional Christians and missional churches do not simply teach about missions, study about missions, and support missions. Missional Christians and churches do missions as their lifestyles. Opportunities for missionary work in God's kingdom exist on every side. It is the task of every Christian; every believer and every church has the responsibility to serve and engage in direct missionary efforts.

Wherever God places you, He places you there as a missionary to share His message and His love with all persons in every group. You are the missionary. You are called of God to commit to and participate in God's worldwide mission.

This book seeks to inspire you to begin the process of becoming a missional Christian and helping your church join the process of becoming a missional church.

In each section, the author provides exercises to guide the reader's thinking and applying of the teachings in that section. Should a reader find the space insufficient, simply write in the margin or on other paper. Should the reader find the space too great for his/her answers, simply use the space needed. The amount of space does not always indicate the amount of material that needs to be written. In most cases, the material the reader writes in the exercises is not right or wrong but the expression of the reader's views.

Introduction

A mission-minded Christian and a mission-minded church occupy a distinct and important place in God's work in this day. A larger and more imperative need, however, exists and must be addressed. *Mission-minded Christians and churches, in this day, need to become missional Christians and missional churches.*

The difference is that mission-minded Christians and churches think about, study about, support, give to, and otherwise place missions central in their lives and ministries. Missional Christians and churches, on the other hand, actually participate in missionary service. Traditionally, Christians and churches delegate missionary service to others and support them while they "do missions." *Missional Christians and churches engage directly and personally in missionary efforts everywhere.*

Traditional missionaries have been sent by the churches to other peoples. These dedicated servants of God have proclaimed the Message of Jesus, led people to salvation, gathered them into congregations, taught them the truth of Christ, and equipped them for service. No one questions the dedication or effectiveness of these noble servants of God.

Today, however, the world critically needs a new approach to missionary activity. Rather than a few specially chosen, sent, and supported workers (missionaries), we need to turn to the approach of missional Christians and churches that participate, personally and directly, in the world mission. Some Christians in the churches can do whatever ministry or work that needs to be done. Missional Christians and churches take the responsibility for worldwide missions as their personal opportunity and calling.

You do not only send missionaries, support missionaries, or pray for missionaries. You may do all of this—but to a larger degree, *you are the missionary.* You will share the message of Jesus with the world and all the people (and peoples) in the world. You will heal the sick, train the believers, guide the congregations, and serve the needy.

Many churches today provide opportunities for mission trips to other areas. These experiences provide avenues for missionary service. In your immediate neighborhood, however, thousands of opportunities await the missionary service of God's people. Take advantage of all mission trips in which you can participate. But do not overlook the missionary work in your own areas.

Missional Christians and churches do missions every day in every place. *You are the missionary.* God's work will flourish as never before, since New Testament times, when God's people become missional and serve as missional Christians in missional churches.

Some years ago, a missionary in Central America, Kenneth Strachan, discovered a principle. He studied the three groups that were growing most rapidly in the Central American country where he served. These groups were the Pentecostals, the Communists, and the Jehovah's Witnesses.

These groups did not have the same message, the same organizational principles, and basically did not follow the same methods. Why, asked Strachan, had the communists in Central America increased to over 915,000,000 in 100 years? How had the Jehovah's Witnesses reached a growth rate of 400%? What led to the growth of the Pentecostals to over 15,000,000 in just 50 years? After intense study, he found one undeniable common factor. Using the discovery of this factor, Strachan developed a principle. Strachan declared:

> "The secret of expansion," said Strachan, was to be found in this thesis: *that the successful expansion of any movement is in direct proportion to its success in mobilizing and occupying its total membership in constant propagation of its beliefs"* (*Evangelism-in-Depth*, 25).

What he taught us is that if we want Christianity to spread across the world, we must find ways to engage our entire body of believers in the constant proclamation of God's truth. We can do exactly this when we move in the direction of the practice of missional Christians in missional churches.

May the Lord of the Harvest call all believers to begin the process of becoming missional Christians and all of the congregations to begin the process of becoming missional churches! Then, we will experience the explosive expansion that the believers in the first century saw as the Gospel spread across the world of their day.

SESSION 1

MISSIONAL CHRISTIANS and CHURCHES: WHAT?

Betty McKnight is a mission-minded Christian. She seldom misses a missionary program at her church. She reads constantly about missionaries and their work. She talks, supports, and prays for missions. She gives beyond her means to offerings for missions. She expresses her interest in and commitment to missions in regular and different ways. Those who know her agree that Betty is a *mission-minded Christian.*

Central City Church is a mission-minded congregation. The church teaches missions and emphasizes missionary efforts and needs on a regular basis. They highlight missionaries and missionary work. The church promotes missionary studies, invites missionary speakers, and provides opportunities for giving to missionary causes. Central City Church often leads the denomination in missionary giving. Members of Central City Church regularly participate in mission trips to serve in many different areas of the world. Central City Church *is a mission-minded congregation!*

Betty and Central City Church are excellent examples of Christians and churches that are centered on the study and support of missions. This characteristic of being mission-minded is important for both Christians and churches. Those believers and congregations who are faithful to their own natures as redeemed persons and groups will naturally be mission-minded.

As important as being *mission-minded* is to Christians and churches, *it is not enough.* Christians and churches must go beyond being mission-minded to become truly and totally **missional.** Christians must become *missional* Christians; Churches must become *missional* churches. The alarming fact is that many believers and congregations are unaware of either the necessity or the possibility of becoming missional. Even more alarming, many Christians do not even know what this term means. Christians who fail to become centered on and active in missions as taught in the Bible fall seriously short of God's expectations for believers and for congregations.

Missional Christians and Churches: The Meaning

Missional is a big word and one we do not hear too often. What exactly does it mean? It obviously is closely related to the word, mission, which is, God's great task and the commission that he has given to his people. God wants all people, everywhere:

- to experience relationship with Him,

- to experience His love and presence,

- to reflect His will for people,

- to perform His services to people.

Christians and churches (missional Christians and churches) exist for the purpose of sharing God's great Message with all peoples and bringing them into relationship with him. Missional Christians and churches demonstrate the following *general qualities*:

- Missional Christians and churches accept God's Mission as their personal responsibilities.

- Missional Christians and churches move beyond the support of missions to acting out or practicing missions in their own worlds.

- Missional Christians and churches personally proclaim the Good News *by word and deed* in their own communities and around the world.

- Missional Christians and churches become like Christ in reaching to serve and help others.

- Missional Christians and churches strive to be incarnational as Christ was. By incarnational we mean one who lives in the midst of a group of people with the intention of serving these people in the name of God.

- Missional Christians and churches see beyond their own needs and maintenance to become the arms Jesus can use to reach to all peoples. They exist to serve and glorify God through proclaiming and demonstrating God's love to all.

- Missional Christians and churches accept God's mission as their reason for living. The Mission is the essence of their existence and practices. They commit fully to fulfilling the mission of God.

Missional Christians and churches seek to teach the true Gospel in ways and terms understandable to the people in the community. The Church, without subscribing to or teaching any false doctrine, seeks to express the Message in the terms and methods that are familiar to the people and that claim the attention of the people in the community. The missional Christian and church plant themselves in the community to share God's love.

A missional Christian has the following characteristics:

- An Authentic Disciple of God in Christ

  A missional Christian is an authentic, growing disciple of God who reached that level through personal commitment and relationship with the Risen Lord, Jesus Christ, and the continuing inward guidance from the Holy Spirit

- Responsive to Redeemed nature

  A missional Christian responds to his/her nature as a redeemed person recognizing that by his/her nature he/she belongs to God and establishing His commission as an integral part of his/her life with Christ

- Consumed by God's Mission

  A missional Christian allows the mission of God to consume him or her to the extent that this mission becomes the all-important passion in life and ministry. The Mission becomes his/hers reason for living.

- Accepts Missionary Status

  A missional Christian accepts that he/she is a missionary, called of God to share the Gospel to all and not simply one who helps send others

- Transformed into a Servant

  A missional Christian willingly and eagerly under-
  takes the process of being transformed into one
  who lives for and serves God in his great task of re-
  deeming the people of the world

- Equipped by the Spirit

  A missional Christian allows himself/herself to be
  equipped by the Spirit and the church to reach out
  and serve all humans in their spiritual and physical
  needs

- Adjusts the Presentation of the Message

  A missional Christian seeks to adjust the presentation of the Message to the people he/she is serving.
  These believers stand ready to make any changes
  needed to further the mission of God and its acceptance by the people.

- A Reproducing Believer

  A missional Christian reproduces himself/ herself by
  bringing others to the commitment to God in Jesus
  Christ and into the experience of His salvation and
  service

- Prioritizes others and service to them

  A missional Christian places highest priority on others and the service to others. These believers put
  self aside and seek to touch others with the love of

God. He/she is one who by word and deed proclaims the love and care of God for all peoples

- Maintains a Growing Relationship with God

  A missional Christian maintains an authentic and growing relationship with God that allows him/her to constantly walk with God in His renewing strength for the Mission

- Lives for Others rather than for self

  A missional Christian lives not for self but to do God's will by reaching and serving the people and peoples of God's world.

A missional Church has the following characteristics:

- Composed of Authentic believers living together in God's love

  A missional church is a congregation or group of authentic believers in Jesus Christ who seek to live together in His love and care and seek mutual growth and service

- Holds High Standards for Members

  A missional church is a congregation that sets and maintains high standards for the behavior and service of members. Membership is not made an easy, costless matter. Members understand up front what is expected.

- Equips and empowers the members

A missional church is a congregation that consciously equips and empowers its members to show the glory of God's love and will to all peoples and all areas of the world

- Places God's Mission at the center

  A missional church is a congregation that places mission at the center of its existence. It sees the mission as in its own neighborhood as well as in other regions

- Communicates the pure, biblical Message

  A missional church is a congregation that seeks to communicate the pure biblical Message in ways understandable to and acceptable for the community. This adaptation seeks to make the Message meaningful in the culture of the community

- Emphasizes reproduction

  A missional church is a congregation that emphasizes reproduction—in believers and in congregations that will in turn reproduce

- Looks beyond local needs

  A missional church is a congregation that looks beyond its own needs to the needs of the communities and the peoples

- Engages in loving service

  A missional church is a congregation that acts in loving service to the peoples of the world

- Willing to set aside any tradition or way of doing that hinders God's work.

  A missional church is a congregation that is ready and willing to set aside any tradition or way of doing things in order to more adequately serve as God's instrument of salvation and help

- Accepts the commission of Expressing God's light and love

  A missional church is a congregation that accepts responsibility for the commission of expressing God's light and love to all peoples in all nations

- Commits to reaching the lost and unchurched

  A missional church is a congregation that commits to reaching the lost and unchurched in their own community and to the ends of the earth

- Accepts the task of helping people and societies around the world

  A missional church is a congregation that accepts its task as helping the people and the societies of the world to become transformed by God's unmerited grace in Jesus Christ.

Missional Christians and missional churches move beyond being mission-minded. They exist as the *instruments of mission* rather than as the *support for missions*. Missional Christians and churches respond to God's call to *be and do* mission rather than being mission-minded. Missional Christians and churches participate directly and

12

personally in mission. Missional Christians and churches consider mission as their DNA, the inner most reality of their being. They exist *because of* the mission not *for* the mission. They accept the responsibility of *fulfilling* God's mission to the world. They will sacrifice whatever is necessary in order to fulfill that mission.

Missional Christians and Churches: The Imperative

We hear much today about the need for missional churches. This emphasis is well-taken and imperative for Christian groups today. God desires that His churches become missional in nature. *We support the movement toward missional churches.*

An integral part of moving toward having missional churches involves developing many missional Christians. *Without missional Christians we can never have missional churches.* In one of the better books on missional churches, Mildred Minatrea, defines a missional church as one that is a congregation that is reproducing through authentic disciples who are being equipped as missionaries sent by God (2004:8). Note that Minatrea says that a missional church is:

- One that reproduces

- One that reproduces by means of authentic disciples

- One that equips the members to be missionaries.

In his statement, Minatrea underlines the truth that a missional church is composed of missional Christians.

While in total agreement with the emphases on missional churches, this guidebook begins with individual believers. *The essence of this book's teaching is that we must begin with missional Christians in order to have missional churches.* This guide seeks to help believers become missional Christians who in turn aid their churches in becoming missional churches.

Missional Christians and Churches: Your Status

Now that we understand at least to a small degree the meanings of missional when related to believers and to congregations, we need to discover to what degree we are missional Christians and to what degree our church is missional. Every Christian and the members of every congregation should analysis themselves and ascertain to what degree they approach being missional. Several exercises that will help understand to what degree we are missional Christians and to what degree our churches are missional congregations.

Exercises for this Session

Throughout this guide, you will find exercises that will help you apply the teachings of the guide. These exercises not only help you be certain you understand the concepts and viewpoints of the guide but even more importantly help you to consider your personal status and that of your church. By carefully using these exercises, you will find many avenues to begin the process of becoming a missional Christian in a missional church.

1. **What differences do you see in "mission-minded" Christians and "missional" Christians?**

The two tables below help you to express the differences between *mission-minded persons and churches* and *missional Christians and churches*. Write in the first table your thinking as to the meaning of mission-minded and missional. In the second table, write other insights you gain from members of the study group if you are in such a group.

Your Understandings

Mission-minded Christian	
Missional Christian	
Mission-minded Church	
Missional Church	

15

Insights from Others

Mission-minded Christian	
Missional Christian	
Mission-minded Church	
Missional Church	

2. To what degree do you think you are a missional Christian and to what degree do you think your church is a missional church?

Estimate and mark on the scales of 1-10 (with 1 being the least) your life and your church as missional

You as a missional Christian

| 1 | 2 | 3 | 4 | 5 | 6 | 7 | 8 | 9 | 10 |

Your Church as a missional Church

| 1 | 2 | 3 | 4 | 5 | 6 | 7 | 8 | 9 | 10 |

What observations led you to the estimates above? Write them below.

3. Write a brief description of a missional Christian or a missional church. It may be an actual person or congregation or it might be one you conceive in your mind.

4. In the spaces below, write in the first section what is needed in your life for you to become a missional Christian. In the second section, write what your church needs to do to become a missional church

For You to Become a Missional Christian	For Your Church to Become a Missional Church

5. Of the characteristics of missional Christians, which seem to you to be the most important? Of the characteristics of missional churches which seem to you to be most important? Write your thinking in the chart below.

Characteristics for Christians	Characteristics for churches

Session 2

Missional Christian and Churches: Why?

Each spring we witness a series of beautiful events on our balcony. Birds nest in what I intended to be hanging flower baskets. They lay eggs, hatch the eggs, feed the baby birds, and eventually teach them to fly and find their own food. It is a fascinating process to watch. The birds have nested on our balcony for three straight years and seem to have become accustomed to us. They go right about their nesting while we work in the flowers on the balcony.

Why do the birds build nests, lay eggs, hatch eggs, and care for their young? They do this because it is the nature of birds to act in this way. Little birds come from eggs placed and tended in nests. Puppies do not come from eggs in nests. Birds respond to their natures and puppies respond to their natures. It is the way God intended it. It is the way He created birds and dogs to act.

God also has a plan for Christians and churches in their spiritual development. This plan involves a spiritual sequence of trusting Christ for salvation, learning to walk with Christ in Christian living and service, and committing to the great mission of sharing the New Life in Christ with the entire world. In other words, *God has created believers and churches in such ways that he intends them to become missional Christians and missional churches.*

God has created his new people to become missional Christians; He created his churches to become missional congregations. Believers who fall below the goal of becoming missional are missing a vital part of God's will and plan. How tragic should the baby birds in the nests never learn to fly.

Congregations that do not become missional churches fall short of God's will and plan for them. The quality of becoming missional is not for the few, especially called Christians and churches. Missional nature is God's intension for *every believer and every congregation.*

Regrettably, many Christians and many congregations never reach this mark of becoming missional. We have intervened in God's plan and placed human barriers in the spiritual process of developing into missional Christians and missional congregations. We have become satisfied with the mediocrity of being less than missional in personal life and in church life. We are failing to become missional Christians and missional churches and the Christian movement is suffering because of this failure. We must find new commitment to becoming missional Christians in missional churches.

Reasons Some Fail to
Become Missional

A normal question arises about our failure to become missional in either our personal lives of the lives of our churches. Why do we remain on a level below missional? Among the many reasons that limit believers and congregations from becoming missional are:

Holding Low Expectations

A major cause of failing to become missional lies in our low expectations. We consider mediocre Christian living and church life to be normal and are satisfied at that level.

We do not reach beyond this state. We expect nothing more than mediocrity. We make entrance into the church easy and ask little from those who come into the fellowship. We substitute being mission-minded for being missional. We send others to be missionary and remain uninvolved personally. We conceive missions to be something done in other lands by special people and do not consider personally engaging in mission ourselves.

Such low expectations seldom result in missional Christians or congregations. Believers in Jesus Christ must have a vision for their lives and service. These believers expect much from themselves and their churches. Their high expectations actually are nothing more than God's intentions. Individual believers and congregations will only become missional as they move beyond the usual low expectations for Christians and churches. A vision for becoming missional is a vastly needed insight for Christians and churches. *What is your expectation for yourself and for your church?*

Exercises for This Section

1. What are your expectations for your church in regard to it becoming a missional church?

_____
_____
_____
_____
_____
_____
_____
_____
_____
_____
_____

2. What signs do you see signs of your church holding low expectations in regard to missional nature?

_____
_____
_____
_____
_____
_____
_____
_____
_____
_____
_____
_____
_____

3. What signs do you see in your personal life that you are accepting low expectations in regard to becoming missional?

_____
_____
_____
_____
_____
_____
_____
_____
_____
_____
_____
_____
_____
_____
_____
_____
_____

Seeing Missions as the
Special Task of the Few

An equally serious mistake that hinders the development of believers and congregations in the quest to become missional is the error of conceiving missions as the task of the few. Missionaries are seen as those responding to "special service" and who go to other lands to proclaim the message. Christians feel that only as they go on "mission trips" are they missionaries.

We have made a false dichotomy between clergy and laity and required missionary efforts only from the former. In fact, in some circles some forms of ministry are restricted to "ordained ministers." Only these "real pastors" are allow to baptize, to administer the Lord's Supper, and to preside at weddings and funerals.

Missional Christianity involves the entire body of Christ actively participating in every phase of the Lord's service. Missions are the responsibility not of the chosen few who are supported by the rest but the task of all believers. Only as every believer and every congregation accepts and acts on the responsibility of fulfilling the mission of God will Christians and churches become missional. *Do you view yourself as a missionary?*

Exercises for This Section

1.   Henry Patterson is a mechanic at an automobile dealership. He leads a small group in a Christian fellowship that meets in a home. Should Henry present the Lord's Supper to the group?

_____
_____
_____
_____
_____

Why or why not?

_____
_____
_____
_____
_____
_____
_____
_____

Should Henry baptize a convert?

_____
_____

Why or why not?

_____
_____
_____
_____

2.   What are ministries in your church and your community that a missional Christian should be filling?

_____
_____
_____
_____

Demanding Our Comfort Zones

Christians and congregations will fall short of becoming missional so long as they demand that they be able to maintain their human-made comfort zones. Christians and churches that refuse to consider new methods and never accept a need for change will seldom reach missional nature. When we insist on our own forms of music, worship, preaching, and service, we often fail to adjust to the new peoples who need the Lord. Refusal to change to meet the needs of local peoples prevents many believers and congregations from becoming missional

Missional Christians and churches never compromise the Bible's teaching. They do however stand ready to adjust the way they present this Message. They do not insist that people become like them but they go to the unchurched in ways that interest and attract these unchurched. Missional Christians and churches are willing to move out of their comfort zones. *What characteristics of your life and the life of your church represent "comfort zones" that you are unwilling to give up?*

Exercises for This Section

1. What evidences do you see in your life and in the life of your church that points to an unwillingness to change in order to reach new people?

_____
_____
_____
_____
_____

2. What recommendations would you make to your church as to the possibilities of changing in order to reach new people?

_____
_____
_____

27

Centering on Maintenance Rather Than Ministry

Maintaining the organization becomes a central focus for too many believers and their churches. This concentration on maintenance eclipses the imperative need for outreach. The Christian and the church seek ways to maintain their "status quo" and miss opportunities to serve others and thereby serve God. Cal Guy, the teacher of missionary methods, was known to say that "status quo" is just a fancy word for "this mess we are in." Keeping existing structures "safe" diverts energy and resources from ministry.

To become missional, Christians and congregations must look outward. They must find their passion in serving others rather than caring for self. They must consider no tradition or accepted pattern as untouchable. Missional Christians and churches accept ministry to others as more important than maintaining their own familiar organizations. Missional Christians are willing to make whatever sacrifices are necessary to meet the spiritual and physical needs of the people. *What percentage of your church's resources is aimed at ministry to others and what percentages of your church's resources are aimed at maintaining the structure?*

Exercises for This Section

1.   What percentage of the budget goes to local expenses for the church's own needs?

2. What could be done to change this situation?

_____

_____

_____

_____

_____

_____

Maintaining Obsolete Institutions

Many Christians and congregations never approach missional nature because they insist on maintaining the institutions and traditions they have always used. Many of these methods and traditions have lost effectiveness. Christians and congregations that cling to out modeled and ineffective traditions minimized their possibilities of becoming missional.

Heights Church had always promoted Sunday Evening Services at the church facility. In recent years, their membership had moved from the central district of the town and located in many different suburban areas. The attendance at these Sunday evening services dwindled partly because of the time demand of the people driving back to the church facility on Sunday evening. Some members who drove almost one hour to get to the church building and one hour home found that to return for the Sunday evening church allowed them only about 3 or 4 hours at home.

A group of church leaders suggested the Sunday Evening activity be held in small groups that would meet in homes across the areas where the people had moved. The suggestion of changing the Sunday Evening activity met resistance and rejection from a majority of the members. These members pointed out that the church had always had Sunday evening services and to change them would reveal some less dedication and commitment on the part of the members. Heights Church decided to maintain the Sunday Evening Service at the facility and saw the numbers of attendees continue to decline.

Eastside Church had a similar problem as Heights Church. Eastside Church, however, elected to follow a different path. They invited persons in various areas of the city to open their homes for Sunday Evening small group activities. They found that over 100 homes gave the invitation. Soon Eastside Church was having over 1200 persons engaging in Sunday Evening activities in these 100 homes. Eastside Church had remodeled an obsolete structure and changed to a dynamic method that the Holy Spirit blessed. In a sense, Eastside Church became a cell-group church.

We sometimes miss the opportunity to become missional by clinging to out modeled, obsolete, decaying structures. This problem can sometimes be fixed by moving to new and more dynamitic models. Every church will not need to make the same move as Eastside Church did. Every church, however, must sincerely and honestly look at its structures and traditions and judge if some have become obsolete. If some structures are found to have become ineffective, the church should seek new methods that could have more effectiveness.

The same procedure can be active in the individual Christian life. Some believers continue the same Christian growth efforts even when these efforts contribute little. They continue the activities because they have been told they should. It often proves that one can make strides in spiritual growth by finding new spiritual exercises and activities. When new patterns of Christian living are suggested, believers should evaluate these methods and if they seem valid try them. Again, clinging to traditional activities sometimes is less effective for Christian growth than finding new means.

Exercises for This Section

1. What methods or institutions in your church seem to be obsolete to you?

_____

_____

2. What new structures would you suggest to take the place of these practices?

_____

_____

_____

Supporting Rather Than Doing Missions

Many Christians and many congregations fail to become missional because they consider supporting missions enough. Missional Christians and churches go beyond *supporting* missions to *doing* missions. Supporting missions is not wrong. Accepting mission support as enough, however, hinders the process of becoming missional as much as any other one factor. Too many talk of evangelism but fail to witness. Too many express a worldwide interest and concern but remain locked into their own little section of the world. Missional living involves personal involvement in missions.

Missional Christians and churches plunge into missionary service. They do missions because they are missionaries. They proclaim the Good News. They seek the lost and unchurched. They care for the needy. They strive to transform the society. They become involved in God's Mission at every level. They do "mission" as well as support "missions." *What actions in your life could be seen as actually doing missions?*

Exercises for This Section

1.   What evidences do you see that indicate you have you been active in supporting missions but not actually doing missions?

_____

_____

_____

2.   What are some ways that you and your church could begin doing missions in your community?

_____

_____

_____

_____

_____

Considering Missions as Only Ministry in Other Regions

A major reason for failing to move toward missional nature is that of considering missions as something done in other regions. The concept of "foreign missions" plants the idea that missions is done "over there." This faulty understanding blocks vision for missions that cry out for service in the local neighborhoods. Mission opportunities exist in every community in every part of the world.

Many Christians have been absorbed in helping missions in other countries and other parts of the world without ever thinking of the mission opportunities right in their own backyards. Some few who vigorously witness and serve on mission trips find little time for missionary work in their own communities. This viewpoint intensifies the separation between "missionaries" who serve in other lands from local Christians who should be about the Master's work.

We all live in a mission field. In a three week period, I visited three stores of the same name in different towns. I found four people from three areas of the Philippines, five people from four areas of India, six people from four areas of Latin America, three people recently come from two areas of Africa, and two other people who recently arrived from European countries. I am certain I did not meet all the newcomers to this land.

Missional Christians and churches see the Mission of God as involving the entire world. They also recognize that the entire world includes their local region. Missional churches regard the people in their own communities as people in need of God. They design plans for reaching these people. *Do you vision "missionaries" as persons who serve God in other cultures and nations?*

Exercises for This Section

1. What do you think are the most serious reasons that many Christians and churches never become missional?

_____
_____
_____
_____
_____

2.   Which of the reasons for failing to become a missional Christian do you think is the most serious
hindrance in your life?

_____
_____
_____
_____
_____
_____

3.   Which of the reasons for failing to become a missional church do you think is the most serious
hindrance in your church?

_____
_____
_____
_____
_____
_____
_____
_____

4.   What evidences of some of the reasons for not becoming missional in your own life and the life of your
church so you observe?

Believers and churches face these reasons for failing to reach missional nature. On the other hand, however, they also have adequate reasons for becoming missional believers and congregations. *The reasons for striving to become missional inspire and challenge believers to begin this exciting spiritual journey.*

Reasons for Becoming Missional Christians and Churches

The reasons for becoming missional exceed the reasons for failing in both number and importance. We turn now to the reasons that individual believers and local congregations strive to move toward the goal of becoming missional.

The question **why become missional** is important and involves at least six actions. The actions are:

- Responding to our Christian DNA that points toward becoming missional

- Seeking to rise to the example of the missional nature of God by allowing the Spirit to develop the qualities of missional nature in us and thus remake us in god-likeness

- Receiving the clear commission of Christ for becoming missional

- Accepting the full realization of the lost condition of the many people in the world and the dire circumstances in which they live

- Acknowledging our failures to become missional in personal experience and church life

- Living in the assurance of the possibilities becoming missional Christians in missional churches.

Why do we strive to be missional Christians and to help our church become a missional church? Why do we strive to allow this characteristic to be developed in us? What truths and motivations drive Christians to engage in the ministries and practices that relate to missional Christianity? We do so because of the following truths.

Our Christian DNA Demands That We Become Missional

Each of us began as a single cell. Within that cell was the DNA that would determine much of what we would become. This DNA would determine if we would be male or female, about how large we would be, what color our hair, skin, and eyes would be, and something of the talents and abilities we would have. While we can improve greatly on many things related to our lives, we cannot change much of what is there in our original DNA.

We will develop as a person in line with our DNA. Biologically, we cannot do otherwise. When we are born again in a transforming, salvation experience, we receive our Christian DNA. This DNA points in the direction we should develop. The problem is that unlike the biological model, we can fail to develop in the direction of our new DNA. We can neglect spiritual things and fail to implement spiritual opportunities.

God's plan for believers and churches is that they become missional. He has written this plan into the DNA of believers and through them into churches. This DNA points to believers and congregations becoming missional. Christians and churches seek to become missional, not because they desire some reward or because they feel some obligation. They seek to become missional because they know inwardly that this character is built into their status as part of the body of Christ. The natures of redeemed persons and redeemed fellowships drive them to allow the Mission of God to become central in and the essence of their lives.

Many Christians and many congregations, however, have become involved in other pursuits and failed to develop in the proper direction of missional nature. They have accepted lesser goals and center on lower values than becoming missional. In such events, the believer and the church move in directions not in keeping with their DNA as redeemed. The problems are obvious.

We should strive to become a missional Christian because that is what God planned us to be and provided for us to become. We should desire our church to become a missional church because that is God's will for the church and is in line with what God built into the church.

A giant negative attaches to this truth that Christian DNA points toward the necessity of becoming missional. Certain aspect of one's DNA determines that that one becomes a tall person. How tall, may depend on environmental factors. But the DNA sets the direction. In the spiritual area, however, believers and congregations can refuse or neglect to move in the missional nature to their ultimate loss.

Believers and congregations should accept the fact that living beneath the missional natures represents a failure to reach God's ideal for believers or congregations. Salvation introduces a believer into a personal relationship with God; proper response to this new nature calls for missional activity. We must also accept the fact that too often we have failed to become missional or even to embark on the journey toward missional nature.

Our relationship with Jesus Christ and the ministry of the Holy Spirit is intended to empower believers to become missional and practice the works of that nature. To fail to do so means to live beneath God's will and desire for that person or church. Living below our newly created nature involves spiritual danger. We must never be satisfied to be less than missional believers in missional congregations.

Christians and churches strive to live up to their natures as children of God and fellowships of God's children. One aspect of living up to this nature is becoming missional. Christians and churches become missional by responding properly to their DNA.

Exercises for This Section

1. Christians and churches strive to reach the characteristic of missional Christians and churches by

_____

_____

_____

_____

38

2.   Christians and churches will reach the level of missional living only by the empowering of the:

_____

_____

_____

_____

_____

The Example of God's Missional Nature Demands We Become Missional

Christians and churches reach toward the level of missional because they recognize the missional quality in the nature of God. We know we can never be like God. We can, however, strive to be made "godly" by the Holy Spirit. As we understand God's great missional nature and desire, this vision stimulates us to become missional and guides our churches to become missional.

God reveals his nature and will to humans. We find the records of this revelation in the Bible. The subject of the missional nature of God is indeed a monumental study. Time and space are not available for describing God's missional nature. We can, however, point in the direction of this teaching and suggest some ways believers and churches can move in the direction of this characteristic.

The Bible teaches that God is eternal, Creator, Living, and in control of the universe. God has no beginning and no ending; He is eternal (Ps. 90:1-2; Neh. 9:5; 1 Tim. 1:17; 6:15-16). God alone created the world and all in it; apart from God nothing exists (Gen. 1:1; Is. 42:5-6; Col.

1:15-16; Rev. 10:5-7). He alone is the Living Lord (Job 19:25; Mt. 16:16; Heb. 10:31). The Living God controls the universe (Gen. 17:1; Lk. 1:37).

No human can or ever will have these powers. We can, with the Spirit's empowering presence, move in the direction of His care for all of creation and dependence on His mighty power, unlimited concern, and unsleeping watch over the world and its people. Missional Christians and congregations accept God eternal, creative, caring power. They seek to live in it and witness by it. The eternal nature of God and His ownership of all lead us to greater determination to become His witnesses and serve others through Him. God's nature calls us to become missional.

Following the example of Christ, who revealed to us what God is like, involves becoming personally and actively engaged in God's mission to the world. As God's people we must become missional Christians in missional churches.

Exercises for This Section

1. Because God loves and desires the salvation of all persons, Christians who strive to follow God's example must also

_____

_____

2. What assurances does the nature of God give you as you strive to love and care for others in this world?

_____

_____

_____

_____

The Bible teaches that God is Father, Love, and Savior. The Bible, in direct statements, reveals that God is love and that His love reaches to all people (Ps. 25:10; Ex. 15:13; Deut 5:10; 1 John 3:1-3; 4:13). God reveals His love for all in the great actions He has done of creation, salvation, and protection of His people (John 3:16; Psalm 23). The great love of God is clearly seen in the tremendous expression of His grace that provides eternal life through Jesus Christ to those who believe (Eph. 2:1-10).

God reveals that His character is that of Father. The Bible is speaking of the nature of a Hebrew father who considers his child as the most important thing in life and commits totally to the wellbeing of the child. God is the Father who cares for his own (Ps. 68:4-6; John 10:1-18). He alone is Savior through Jesus Christ (1 Tim. 2:3-4; John 3:16-21, 36). God has revealed, by word and by deed, that He is love, Father, and Savior.

Based on the nature of God as loving, Father, and Savior, Christians should strive to develop the characteristics of love for others, care for others, and witnesses, sharing the Good News with others (1 John 3:16-20; 4:7-12; John 15: 9-17). We are commissioned by God's love to love others and share the Good News with them (2 Cor. 5: 11-21). God's nature becomes an example for us to love, care for, and share with all people.

Exercises for This Section

1.   What types of deeds can you do that would show others the Love of God?

_____

_____

_____

41

_____

_____

2.   What characteristics did Jesus indicate in His life
      that demonstrated the great love of God?

_____

_____

_____

3.   Is it possible for a church to demonstrate the love of
      God? How?

_____

_____

_____

_____

The Bible teaches that God's Nature is servanthood.
In biblical teaching, servanthood is the highest, strongest,
and noblest of characteristics. Servanthood is in no way low
or demeaning. Servant leadership and service demands the
strongest of Christian efforts.

One of the plainest teachings of servanthood comes
directly from the teachings of Jesus in John 12:20-37.

> *Now there were some Greeks among those who went up to
> worship at the Feast. They came to Philip, who was from
> Bethsaida in Galilee, with a request. "Sir," they said, "we would
> like to see Jesus." Philip went to tell Andrew; Andrew and Philip
> in turn told Jesus.*
>
> *Jesus replied, "The hour has come for the Son of Man to be
> glorified. I tell you the truth, unless a kernel of wheat falls to
> the ground and dies, it remains only a single seed. But if it
> dies, it produces many seeds. The man who loves his life will
> lose it, while the man who hates his life in this world will keep
> it for eternal life. Whoever serves me must follow me; and*

where I am, my servant also will be. My Father will honor the one who serves me.

"Now my heart is troubled, and what shall I say? 'Father, save me from this hour'? No, it was for this very reason I came to this hour. Father, glorify your name!"

Then a voice came from heaven, "I have glorified it, and will glorify it again." The crowd that was there and heard it said it had thundered; others said an angel had spoken to him.

Jesus said, "This voice was for your benefit, not mine. Now is the time for judgment on this world; now the prince of this world will be driven out. But I, when I am lifted up from the earth, will draw all men to myself." He said this to show the kind of death he was going to die (John 12:20-32 NIV).

In this passage, Jesus told His disciples (and us as well) that the only way to produce genuine fruit is through dying to self. Dying to self means placing the will of God and the needs of others in first place in our lives. It means living for God and for others. It means moving beyond thinking of ourselves and our needs to thinking of others. It means seeking the welfare of others rather than our own advancement. It means laying aside any ambitions that might lead us to compromise the truth of God or our service to Him. It means a willingness to die to self for the service of God and others.

Christians and churches that desire to move toward missional character accept the goal of living as servants. Jesus indicated that His plan for His people is servanthood. Jesus explained to His followers that His plan for them was not to impress or control others but rather to serve others. Followers of Jesus, like the Lord Himself did, be willing to give themselves as a ransom for others. Jesus taught,

When the ten heard about this, they were indignant with the two brothers. Jesus called them together and said, "You know

43

that the rulers of the Gentiles lord it over them, and their high officials exercise authority over them. Not so with you. Instead, whoever wants to become great among you must be your servant, and whoever wants to be first must be your slave— just as the Son of Man did not come to be served, but to serve, and to give his life as a ransom for many" (Matt 20:24-28 NIV).

To become great in the Kingdom of God, that is, to reach God's will, is to become a servant of all. Missional Christians and Churches seek ways to help others and serve them. Missional Christians overcome (by the ministry of the Holy Spirit) the desire to control or use others. Missional Christians and congregations pursue the characteristic of servants.

Exercises for This Section

1.   How do you understand the characteristic of servanthood? Write your view below.

_____

_____

_____

_____

2.   Write an illustration of a Christian who exhibits servanthood

_____

_____

_____

_____

_____

The Bible teaches that God has the power to reach His purposes. God's power is not limited as human abilities are limited. God knows all, is in all places, and possesses all power. These qualities are often expressed as God is omniscient, omnipresent, and omnipotent.

A wonderfully comforting and strengthening truth resides in these revelations of God's nature. God knows all things but more importantly is the truth that God knows me. God is everywhere but even more strengthening is the fact that God is where I am and beside me in my needs. God is all-powerful but more important God has the power to care for me (Ps. 139; Matt. 28:16-20; Acts 1:8).

For believers who desire to become missional Christians and congregations who desire to become missional churches, *the power of God assures that the level of missional nature is possible*. It is possible not by human effort but by God's unquestioned power. Christians and congregations can become missional because the Holy Spirit will impart to them the capacities to reach this level of life. Every believer can become a missional Christian because of the unquestioned and unlimited power of God that is available to these believers.

Exercises for This Section

1. Do you ever question your abilities to reach God's will and become a missional Christian?

_____

_____

_____

_____

2. What assurances do you have that you can become a missional Christian and that your church can become a missional church?

_____

_____

The Bible teaches that God desires the Salvation of all people in the world. God desires that not one perish (Isa. 48:5-6; 53:6; Matt. 28:16-20; Acts 1:8; 1 Tim 2: 1-7. The Old Testament proclaims God's desire that His people share His salvation with all people.

> *And now the LORD says —*
> *he who formed me in the womb to be his servant*
> *to bring Jacob back to him*
> *and gather Israel to himself,*
> *for I am honored in the eyes of the LORD*
> *and my God has been my strength —*
> *he says:*
> *"It is too small a thing for you to be my servant*
> *to restore the tribes of Jacob*
> *and bring back those of Israel I have kept.*
> **I will also make you a light for the Gentiles,**
> **that you may bring my salvation to the ends of the ear***th"*
> *(Isa 49:5-6 NIV).*

The Old Testament also teaches that God has provided His salvation for all.

> *We all, like sheep, have gone astray,*
> *each of us has turned to his own way;*
> *and the LORD has laid on him*
> *the iniquity of us all* (Isa 53:6 NIV)

In the Great Commission we have already studied, Jesus commissioned His followers to make disciples of "all" peoples. These words refer to groups of people but it includes every person as well. God desires the salvation of all people.

As Jesus commissioned His people at the beginning of the movement to reach all peoples, He spoke to them of becoming His witnesses in Jerusalem, in Galilee, in Samaria, and to the uttermost parts of the world (Acts 1:8). His plan obviously includes all people, everywhere. His plan also includes all believers be active and involved in the teaching of His message to all peoples.

The Apostle Paul emphasized God's will that all be saved as he wrote:

> *I urge, then, first of all, that requests, prayers, intercession and thanksgiving be made for everyone— for kings and all those in authority, that we may live peaceful and quiet lives in all godliness and holiness. **This is good, and pleases God our Savior, who wants all men to be saved and to come to a knowledge of the truth. For there is one God and one mediator between God and men, the man Christ Jesus**, who gave himself as a ransom for all men — the testimony given in its proper time. And for this purpose I was appointed a herald and an apostle — I am telling the truth, I am not lying — and a teacher of the true faith to the Gentiles* (1 Tim 2:1-7 NIV, emphasis mine).

No doubt exists as to God's desire and plan. All people are in His desire and plan. So must all people be in the desire of God's people. Missional Christians and congregations have this same desire and participate in this plan.

Exercises for This Section

1.   Write the names of several people you know who are in need of God's salvation

_____

_____

_____

_____

2.   Write the names of the people you hope to reach for Christ in your own neighborhood and in the place you will be serving outside your neighborhood

_____

_____

_____

_____

The Bible teaches that God will be with His people as they serve in His mission.

No Christian and no congregation is asked to take up God's mission in only human strength. Jesus promises to be with His people on mission. This assurance should help believers and congregations seek to become missional Christians and Churches.

The example of the missional nature of God, therefore, incites us to seek to become missional Christians and to help our churches become missional congregations. The truth as to God's unlimited power guides us in the efforts to become missional in that we know that adequate power for the job exists.

We do not have the power but He does. He has promised to empower us so that we can lead the unsaved and the unchurched to faith and responsible living. Jesus sent out the 72 witnesses with instructions to spread the Message. These commissioned believers returned to report that the Holy Spirit had granted to them abilities to proclaim Christ far beyond any powers they had (Mt. 10:1-17).

The matter of highest importance in this discussion of the missional nature of God is the truth that as believers, we are to follow God's example to the degree that this level of living is possible. We will never be God nor will we ever perfectly mirror His purity, love, and faithfulness. But godly living is our goal. The Spirit works to empower us in the pilgrimage to become like God in our daily lives. The more godly we become the more we will participate as missional Christians in missional churches.

God's Commission Demands
We Become Missional

The mission of Christians and churches begins in the heart of God; it is not of human origin. No group of persons conceives of the mission and places it on Christians or churches. The commission is uniquely from God; His people strive to fulfill this commission in His power.

The commission indicates that God desires and expects His people to serve the entire world, witness to every person and group of persons, lead them to saving faith and eternal life, and serve them faithfully in the Name of Christ. The Commission began in the Garden where God came seeking the fallen pair (Gen. 3:8-9).

We have already seen how God spoke to the Prophet Isaiah and revealed God's desire for all peoples (49:5-6). Jesus noted the worldwide nature of the Mission as He spoke with His followers after His Resurrection. He indicated that they would be empowered by the Holy Spirit and become His witnesses in Jerusalem, in Judea, in Samaria, and to the ends of the earth (Acts 1:8). These geographical areas are of course both literal and figurative. The emphasis is that the field is the entire world.

Jesus gave the fullest statement of the Commission in what has become known as "The Great Commission." Jesus said:

Then the eleven disciples went to Galilee, to the mountain where Jesus had told them to go. When they saw him, they worshiped him; but some doubted. Then Jesus came to them and said, "All authority in heaven and on earth has been given to me. **Therefore go and make disciples of all nations**, *baptizing them in the name of the Father and of the Son and of the Holy Spirit, and teaching them to obey everything I have commanded you. And surely I am with you always, to the very end of the age* (Matt 28:16 NIV).

The Great Commission teaches that:

- The Mission comes from Jesus who has the authority and the right to send us on Mission

- The Mission is to make disciples. Going is not the primary commission but leading the lost to an experience with the Living Lord and a continuing walk with Him is the heart of the Commission

- The Mission includes guiding people to acknowledge their faith (baptizing)

- The Mission includes guiding people to full understanding of God's way (teaching them)

- The Mission is directed at *all* the peoples of the earth

- The Mission is carried out with the constant presence and protection of the Holy Spirit

The Commission is for all Christians, not only a few specially called and sent individuals. It is not limited to disciples or to regions but includes all believers and all parts of the world. It was to the entire Jerusalem Fellowship that the Risen Christ commissioned His followers to a worldwide Mission (Acts 1:8).

The fourth reason for striving to become missional Christians in missional churches is the clear an unequivocal commission from God to His people. Missional believers and congregations are on Mission. They support missions but even more so the engage in missions. Missional Christians are missionaries; missional churches are fellowships on mission. The Mission is their reason for existence and the primary impulse of their lives. They exist to carry out the Commission of God in Christ and by the empowering of the Holy Spirit.

Exercises for This Section

1. To whom is the Great Commission given?

_____

_____

_____

2. What actions or services does the Great Commission instruct missional Christians and churches to do?

_____

_____

_____

_____

_____

_____

3. Complete the diagram of the words of the Great Commission (Your instructor may help you with this diagram).

The Frightening Condition Of the Lost and Unchurched Demands We Become Missional

A fifth reason for striving to become a missional Christian and a missional congregation is the plain biblical teaching that every person without Jesus Christ and His salvation is lost. Those who are without Christ and lost have neither the assurance of Heaven after death or the loving presence and blessing of living in Christ now. The terrible plight of the unsaved drives believers to missional service.

Jesus is not simply the best Savior; He is the only Savior. We find good teachings and noble thoughts in other religions. Other faiths give wise counsel on ways to live and associate with others. We perceive beauty and proper guidance in the teachings of other religions. Salvation and eternal life come, however, only through a personal commitment to the Historic Christ by means of an experience during one's lifetime.

This teaching seems harsh or unfair to many. The truth is that God offers His salvation to every person and desires that all will come to repentance and faith. Many around the world, however, resist His gracious offer and decline His loving invitation. The truth remains that salvation and eternal life can be received only through God's Son, Jesus Christ.

Jesus taught directly that He is the only "way" to eternal life:

> *Jesus answered, "I am the way and the truth and the life. No one comes to the Father except through me. If you really knew me, you would know my Father as well. From now on, you do know him and have seen him"* (John 14:6-7 NIV).

52

The Apostles confirmed this teaching as they spoke to the people in Jerusalem at the Temple:

Salvation is found in no one else, for there is no other name under heaven given to men by which we must be saved (Acts 4:12 NIV).

Peter acknowledged that the Roman soldier, Cornelius, was a good man who tried to follow the commands of the Living God. Cornelius, however, was not in the family of God. He needed the Word of salvation that Peter brought. The goodness of the life of Cornelius did not provide salvation. That came only by the Word of Jesus Christ. Does this account give us some hope that any person who sincerely seeks God will receive the Message and hope for salvation? (Acts 10:1-48).

The Apostle Paul longed for the salvation of his fellow Jewish people. They were religious and practiced many religious rituals and did many good acts. They did not, however, have salvation in Jesus Christ. Paul wrote:

Brothers, my heart's desire and prayer to God for the Israelites is that they may be saved. *For I can testify about them that they are zealous for God, but their zeal is not based on knowledge. Since they did not know the righteousness that comes from God and sought to establish their own, they did not submit to God's righteousness. Christ is the end of the law so that there may be righteousness for everyone who believes* (Rom 10:1-4 NIV).

Obviously, although the Jewish religious leaders were religious and even faithful in religious acts, they were not saved. Being religious and faithfully following the teachings of some religion does not bring salvation.

Other passages could be given but these few proclaim the central teaching of Scripture—salvation and eternal life come only through Jesus Christ. Those who follow other religions or who are non-religious (Atheists, Materialists) remain outside the safety and blessing of God's Kingdom. *Only Jesus is Savior and one needs only Jesus to be saved.*

Those outside God's salvation in Christ are not only in danger of not reaching Heaven. They also suffer from not having the wonderful blessings of being in Christ and His salvation right now. Paul revealed the vast difference between the saved and the unsaved when he wrote:

> *As for you, you were dead in your transgressions and sins, in which you used to live when you followed the ways of this world and of the ruler of the kingdom of the air, the spirit who is now at work in those who are disobedient. All of us also lived among them at one time, gratifying the cravings of our sinful nature and following its desires and thoughts. Like the rest, we were by nature objects of wrath. But because of his great love for us, God, who is rich in mercy, made us alive with Christ even when we were dead in transgressions — it is by grace you have been saved. And God raised us up with Christ and seated us with him in the heavenly realms in Christ Jesus, in order that in the coming ages he might show the incomparable riches of his grace, expressed in his kindness to us in Christ Jesus. For it is by grace you have been saved, through faith — and this not from yourselves, it is the gift of God—not by works, so that no one can boast. For we are God's workmanship, created in Christ Jesus to do good works, which God prepared in advance for us to do* (Eph 2:1-10 NIV).

Various viewpoints exist today concerning the condition of those who have not received Christ as their only savior. Universalists teach that everyone will be saved eventually. God will not, they teach, allow any to remain separated from Him for eternity. *While this viewpoint would be comfortable, we cannot accept it.* Jesus indicated that some would choose the path that leads to destruction (Mt. 7:13-14). The disturbing fact is that some will not be saved.

Other teachers offer what the call the "wider-hope views." These teachings declare that people must have Christ to be saved. People can, however, they say, find Christ in the other religions. Buddhists, New Age Followers, Muslims, followers of Hinduism, Mormons, and believers in all other religions can find Christ in their own faiths.

The teachers of the wider-hope views point to a passage in the Bhagavad-Gita, the Hindu Holy Book that declares that by whatever path people seek God, God will be found. All roads, they say, lead to God.

Some teachers of "wider hope" even declare that persons will receive opportunity to repent and believe after death. This view, called post-mortem opportunity for salvation, has no basis in Scripture. Christians cannot accept any of the "wider hope theories." These beliefs are human-made, deceptive, and false.

Our belief is that Jesus is the only savior. We know also, that Jesus alone is needed for salvation—we need not add anything, baptism, church membership, the Mass, and any special expression of religious life. Baptism, church membership, a Christian walk all are important but do not in themselves bring salvation. They demonstrate the reality of the salvation that comes by Grace and by Faith and not by works.

The Christian Message is *Only Jesus and Jesus Only*. Jesus is the only Savior; He cannot be found in other religions. Jesus is all that is required for salvation; we need nothing other than faith in Jesus. No requirement of the Mass, some special Christian practice, or pilgrimage to some religious site is necessary for salvation.

Christians seek to move along the process of becoming missional and congregations seek to become missional because they know people without Jesus Christ are lost. The lost do not have the guidance and blessing of living with Jesus now and they have no hope of Heaven. Over five billion people in the world today are without Christ. This sobering fact demands that believers become missional Christians in missional churches.

Over 6,274,189,196 live in the world today (2007). Of these, one estimate is that 32.5 percent are Christian. This figure, however, includes Catholics, Orthodox, Marginal, and people in other groups who are most likely not actually personal believers in Jesus Christ. When adjusted for Christians who most likely are genuine believers, we would arrive at a figure of 15.16 % actually Christians. This would mean that well over 5 billon people have not trusted in Christ and found life in Him today. This sobering fact demands missional nature and activity on the part of all Christians on the face of the earth.

Believers should also remember that lostness brings tragedy to life now as well as in the eternity beyond. The unsaved person has no hope for life in Heaven. He/she also does not have the presence and empowering of Christ during life in the present. The great loss of comfort, peace, service, and strength that Christ gives daily is a matter of greatest importance. The unsaved do not have this tremendous leadership in their lives.

Are you and your church active in seeking to find and win the lost and unchurched? What is the ratio between number of members and number of people who are being saved in your church? Are you guiding people to the wonderful and full life in Christ?

Exercises for This Section

1. If someone says to you that he/she is a very religious person but not a Christian, how do you share with him/her?

_____
_____
_____
_____
_____
_____
_____
_____
_____
_____
_____

2.   Biblical Christianity and Other Views of Salvation
(Write in the spaces provided your understanding of the teachings of each group on salvation and in the third space write your evaluation of that viewpoint)

Viewpoint	Teaching	Evaluation
Universalism		
Wider-Hope		
Biblical		

3.   Using the Passages cited in this chapter, write in the
      column on the left the assurances that Christians
      have and in the column on the right the condition of
      unbelievers

      (These facts are most easily seen in Eph. 2:1-10)

Assurances of Christians	Condition of the Lost

4.   How does Paul's expression of desire for the salva-
      tion of his fellow Jews relate to the teachings of
      salvation in other religions?

_____

_____

_____

_____

_____

5. The Christian teaching on salvation is stated:

Jesus   Only

Our Realizations of Having Failed to Achieve Missional Living Demands We Seek to Become Missional

Christians and churches generally acknowledge that they have failed to achieve missional levels of living and ministry. Knowing that such living is God's will for and plan for believers and congregations, Christians and churches are led to genuine repentance. The confession of past failures to become fully missional does not discourage nor defeat believers. The knowledge of this shortage stimulates true believers to renewed efforts to become missional

Becoming fully missional is a vision and goal that will remain constantly out in front of believers. As believers and congregations move closer to missional levels of living, they will understand more of what such living would involve. They will then be driven to acknowledge they continue to be far from the goal. The goal of missional living for Christian and church remains a constant force drawing both to higher planes of living and service.

As Believers we must strive to become fully missional in life and service. As churches, we must seek to help our congregations become fully missional. Thus, we experience God's constant motivation to become missional.

Exercises for This Section

1. **Explain by writing below, how our past failures to become missional provide constant motivation for seeking such living and service.**

_____
_____
_____

_____

_____

2. Write your commitment to becoming a missional Christian

_____

_____

_____

The Possibility of Becoming Missional Demands We Reach for the Level

Becoming a missional Christian and a missional church is not an impossible mission. The level is fully reachable, not in the strength or ability of any Christian but by the empowering presence of Christ in the believer's life. We often hear quoted that we should become His witnesses in Jerusalem, Judea, Galillee, and to the uttermost parts of the world (Acts 1:8). We sometimes forget that the Risen Christ said, before He commanded the Mission, that His followers receive power when the Holy Spirit came upon them (Acts 1:8).

Clearly, God promises His power for the believer who embarks on the journey of sharing the Word. Jesus' promise in Acts 1 became God's reality in Acts 2. The disciples, gathered in one accord, experienced the infilling power of the Spirit. As one evidence that this miraculous filling had actually happened, the disciples were able to proclaim the Message in words understandable by all the different groups of Jews who were in Jerusalem. Many of these Jews had come from other regions where they spoke languages other than Hebrew. In a miraculous expression of God's power, the believers delivered the Message in words that each person, from every region, could understand (Acts 2:5-12).

We do not know how this miracle happened. Did the Spirit allow these believers from Judea and Galillee to actually speak foreign languages that they did not know? Did the Spirit allow the people to speak in language unknown but that by miracle became understandable by all? We do not know the method but we hear the result. Everyone understood the wonderful story of Salvation.

We know that we can become missional Christians. We know our churches can become missional congregations. We know these possibilities exist because we know it is God's will that it happen. In the book of Acts, we read of the Gospel exploding across the land. Souls flooded to the Truth. Salvation came to thousands. Such "in gatherings" are still possible. Missional Christians and missional churches can and will develop. It is possible in God's tremendous power.

The very possibility of becoming missional Christians in missional congregations drives us to accept God's infilling. The possibility demands the effort. We can become missional and our churches can become missional. We must, therefore, submit to God's guidance and allow His Spirit to develop in us the qualities of missional Christians and missional churches.

Exercises for This Section

1. What biblical truths make you certain that believers today can become missional Christians?

_____

_____

_____

_____

_____

_____
_____
_____

2.   Believers and churches do not become missional by human strength and effort but only by

_____
_____
_____
_____

3.   By way of review, write the reasons for Christians and churches to strive to become missional

_____
_____
_____
_____
_____
_____
_____
_____
_____
_____
_____
_____
_____
_____

Session 3

Missional Christians and Churches: How?

Knowing that God wills that His people and His churches become missional in character immediately raises the question, "How?" Like most Christian growth, missional character will not come automatically. Believers and churches will of necessity respond to the leadership of God through the Holy Spirit in order to become more missional in their natures.

This guide for Christians and churches seeking to become more missional, therefore, now turns to the question: *How do believers and churches become missional?*

By Recognizing the Path to Missional Nature is a Process

Becoming missional is a process. It is not, however, an automatic process. Although written into the DNA of Christians and churches, believers and congregations must submit to God's empowering and exert effort to gain this point of development. The biblical sequence is: salvation through faith in Christ, growth in the development of a Christian walk, involvement in God's mission, and becoming missional in nature.

Becoming missional can be an all-at-once experience but usually involves growth and development over a period of time. Becoming a missional Christian and a missional church follows a process by which God empowers through the ministry of the Holy Spirit. Christians have power to over come sin, according to the Apostle Paul. But we must note that Paul indicates that it is *"by the Spirit"* that we overcome sin (Rom. 8:12-17). Believers and churches can become missional. Becoming missional is, however, achieved by following a well-defined process.

This process calls for one to be sure of his/her salvation. It then, prescribes that one begin the journey of obedience in the development of a Christian walk. By Christian walk I mean a life of growing relationship with Jesus and the increasing observance of His teachings. This pathway eventually can lead to one's becoming a missional Christian.

Exercises for This Section

1. Write your testimony concerning your journey in the process of becoming a missional Christian

_____

_____

_____

_____

2. How far along the process of becoming missional do you think you are?

_____

_____

_____

_____

_____

_____

_____

_____

3.   What do you most need to continue the process of becoming a missional Christian?

_____

_____

_____

_____

_____

_____

_____

By Committing to the Process of Becoming Missional

God gives a missional spirit to those Christians and to those congregations that genuinely desire such a development in their lives. The process of becoming missional is fully the work of God within the believer and the church. No person can reach the level of missional and no church can reach the level of missional by human efforts.

While becoming missional is a godly initiative, the believer and the church must be receptive and committed to the process. God will not overrule a believer's decision in regard to becoming missional. God will woo the believer but not force the believer or a church to become missional. The believer and the church must commit to the process before the Holy Spirit will empower that believer or church. Just as God saves no person apart from that person's repentance and faith in Him, God brings no unwilling believer or church to a missional level.

The clear indication is, therefore, that believers and churches must commit to the process of becoming a missional Christian and a missional church. Apart from such commitment, the process of becoming missional will not happen. God works within the lives of believers and churches only when there is solid commitment on the parts of those believers and congregations.

The call from God is, "Commit to the process of becoming missional." Becoming a missional Christian and becoming a missional church eventuates only when commitment meets God's empowerment. Without your commitment and the commitment of your church to become missional, this state will never be reached. *Have you and your church committed to becoming missional? What will be necessary for you and your church to reach this commitment?*

Exercises for This Section

1. Write your commitment to becoming a missional Christian

_____
_____
_____
_____

2. Write you commitment to helping your church become a missional Church

_____
_____
_____
_____
_____
_____
_____

By Training in Ways of Becoming Missional

In most endeavors, one who contributes invests heavily in training. Training does not insure effectiveness in ministry but a lack of training most often leads to a loss in effectiveness. Christians and churches that desire missional ministry must seek and experience sound training both for the believers and for the churches.

Training in Spiritual Disciplines

Training for missional living and service demands believers seek out specific training for spiritual life and ministry. This training involves developing spiritual disciplines in the believers' lives. By spiritual disciplines I mean those elements that contribute to a spiritual walk with God in Jesus Christ.

The Christian life is often described as a walk with God. It involves expressing daily in all that we do and say the love of God. It is by expressing *in word and* deed the kindness and concern of God for every person. It is recognizing and avoiding all those attitudes, thoughts, and actions that detract from one's character as a child of God. It is recognizing and seeking to fulfill all the attitudes, thoughts, and actions that express one's character as a child of God.

Both Jesus and Paul expressed the attitudes, thoughts, and actions that do not belong in the Christian life of walk and those that are part of this walk. Read these two passages printed below and note what Jesus and Paul teach as matters that do not and do belong in the Christian walk with God. Jesus said:

Again Jesus called the crowd to him and said, "Listen to me, everyone, and understand this. Nothing outside a man can make him 'unclean' by going into him. Rather, it is what comes out of a man that makes him 'unclean.'"

After he had left the crowd and entered the house, his disciples asked him about this parable. "Are you so dull?" he asked. "Don't you see that nothing that enters a man from the outside can make him 'unclean'? For it doesn't go into his heart but into his stomach, and then out of his body." (In saying this, Jesus declared all foods "clean.")

He went on: "What comes out of a man is what makes him 'unclean.' For from within, out of men's hearts, come evil thoughts, sexual immorality, theft, murder, adultery, greed, malice, deceit, lewdness, envy, slander, arrogance and folly. All these evils come from inside and make a man 'unclean' (Mark 7:14-23 NIV).

The Apostle Paul declared:

So I say, live by the Spirit, and you will not gratify the desires of the sinful nature. For the sinful nature desires what is contrary to the Spirit, and the Spirit what is contrary to the sinful nature. They are in conflict with each other, so that you do not do what you want. But if you are led by the Spirit, you are not under law.

The acts of the sinful nature are obvious: sexual immorality, impurity and debauchery; idolatry and witchcraft; hatred, discord, jealousy, fits of rage, selfish ambition, dissensions, factions and envy; drunkenness, orgies, and the like. I warn you, as I did before, that those who live like this will not inherit the kingdom of God.

But the fruit of the Spirit is love, joy, peace, patience, kindness, goodness, faithfulness, gentleness and self-control. Against such things there is no law. Those who belong to Christ Jesus have crucified the sinful nature with its passions and desires. Since we live by the Spirit, let us keep in step with the Spirit. Let us not become conceited, provoking and envying each other (Gal 5:16-6:1 NIV).

68

Exercises for This Section

1. In the chart below, write those characteristics or sinful matters that do not belong in the Christian life

Characteristics and Actions that Do not Belong in the Christian Life

2. In the Chart below, write those characteristics and actions that should be in the Christian life

Characteristics and Actions that should be in the Christian life

The Christian walk is one of beauty, joy, guidance, support, and spiritual health. No other walk can compare with the Christian way. Christians continually thank God for the joys of living and walking with Him. The privileges of walking daily with Jesus and through Him overcoming the damaging ways of the world are some of God's great blessings. Serving others as one continues this walk with God is likewise a tremendous blessing from God.

The Christian walk with God begins with the experience of salvation in Jesus Christ. This experience grants to one Eternal Life. The Christian walk, however, is not just about Heaven. It is that. The Christian walk also involves daily experience with God in Christ, guidance in life, support in life, assurance in life, and joy in life. The unsaved miss the assurance of Heaven. They also miss the joy of living the Christian life here on earth.

How does a believer reach the development of the Christian walk? The obvious means of prayer, Bible Study, worship, and Christian fellowship certainly help and should never be neglected. Believers who desire to live the Christian life should strive to recognize and resist those negative features of life as mentioned by Jesus and Paul in the passages above. Believers should also strive to incorporate, by the power of the Spirit, those attitudes, thoughts, and actions that are part of God's will for His people.

No one method will assure that this walk will become a reality. Every believer will respond in a different way. God will, however, grant to every sincere seeker the development of the characteristics of the Christian walk. As believers recognize their needs, the Holy Spirit will fill them and grant them the victories they need to continue the walk with God.

Exercises for This Section

1. What do you think are the most serious temptations to turn away from God's walk in your life?

_____
_____
_____
_____
_____
_____
_____
_____

2. What are the most needed characteristics in your life for you to deepen your walk with God?

_____
_____
_____
_____
_____
_____
_____

3. Write a prayer asking God to help you with the matters in the last two exercises.

_____
_____
_____
_____

Many books and seminars seek to guide believers in deepening their spiritual walk with the Lord. These resources greatly help one develop his/her spiritual life. Use these resources to deepen your daily walk with Jesus. The Holy Spirit will answer every sincere desire for spiritual growth. A missional Christian and a missional Church reaches the goals the Lord has for them only through the spiritual walk. The beginning place for developing into a missional Christian and a missional Church involves a constant deepening of the spiritual life.

Training in Strategy Development

Strategy sets out the general goals of the mission. In the strategy the leaders of mission set forth the general, overall goals and plans for the mission. The strategy may include the primary ways this effort will be projected.

Statements of strategy might include such concepts as:

- The mission will provide a contextualized witness to the specific group of persons in a particular region

- The mission will lead the people in starting local congregations that fit the culture of the people

- The mission will seek to meet the particular social and human needs of the people

- The mission will teach the people some particular skills needed by the people.

Strategy will be patterned for the needs and the cultures of the peoples to be served. Those seeking to evangelize and serve should not seek methods that fulfill their desires and cultures. They seek the methods that fit the cultures of those they serve. These strategies will outline the goals and purposes of the mission.

Churches have received teaching of the importance of writing a purpose statement. In this statement, the church declares what it plans, in the empowering of the Holy Spirit, to accomplish. Every Christian should also have a purpose statement. What do you, as a believer in Christ, plan to become and to do in His power?

Exercises for This Section

1.   Write you personal purpose statement. Remember, you will reach this purpose only in the empowering of God's Holy Spirit.

_____

_____

_____

_____

_____

_____

_____

_____

2.   With your leaders, sketch out your overall strategies for the mission

_____
_____
_____
_____
_____
_____
_____

3.   What are primary needs in the peoples your mission
      will serve?

_____
_____
_____
_____
_____

4.   How will you know if you have fulfilled the plans of
      your strategies?

_____
_____
_____
_____
_____

Training in Missionary Methods

Methods are the precise plans to reach the goals of the strategies. Missionary methods do not convert people or lead to church starting. The methods God's people use neither assure of fruitfulness nor prevent the Holy Spirit's work. God can fulfill His purposes in spite of our poor methods; our methods do not insure His fruit.

Methods are, however, important in opening the ways for conversion and church starting. The Holy Spirit works through better methods. Believers will not depend on methods. They will, however, seek to allow the Holy Spirit to guide them to the methods that the Spirit can best use to bring people to salvation and to develop congregations in accordance with His will.

Missional Christians will seek the better methods for achieving their purposes. Sometimes, we can read about methods others use and adapt these methods for our service. Sometimes God will lead us directly to the better ways of doing His work. Missional Christians are ever on the lookout for ways of doing God's work but never depend on any of the methods to accomplish the purpose. Accomplishing the purpose of God depends solely on the power of God.

Exercises for This Section

1.   What are the major differences between Strategy and Methods in missionary service?

_____
_____
_____
_____
_____
_____
_____
_____

2.   Write any questions or concerns you have about the methods you may use in your missionary efforts

Training in Cultural Adjustment

The people you will serve on your mission may live in a very different cultural setting than you live in. In order for your mission to reach its desired goals, you will need to design your methods and your goals to fit the local culture. Without surrendering any Christian or biblical truth, you will need to design your proclamation and your ways of teaching to match local ways. Even the churches you start will need to fit the local patterns so far as possible.

A church made up of affluent, well-educated, community leaders felt led to start a new congregation in a neighborhood populated by poor, uneducated, under paid persons. The idea of starting the new congregation was sound. The problem that developed, however, rested on the fact that the affluent church tried to start a congregation patterned exactly like the mother church. The features of the mother church did not fit the people in the new neighborhood. The new church never became strong because it never fit the natures of the people it was to serve.

Missionary methods, whether for a culture in the non-Western World or in the West, must fit the ways of life of the people who are being served. Culture is defined as the way of life or map of a people's belief and practices. Culture is a way of life but only one way of life. Culture molds how people in a certain group view life, respond to life, decide what is right or wrong, what is good to eat, how to dress, what customary actions to follow, and what ways relating to others are proper.

Missionary methods must conform to biblical teachings and never compromise these principles. At the same time, missionary methods should teach people to become Christian in their own cultures and practice the Christian life in their own settings. The goal is conversion without cultural dislocation. People should be led to come to Christ and walk in the Christian way and remain in contact with their own people and cultures. This cultural adjustment is one of the most creative activities of missionaries.

Christian conversion will of necessity lead to cultural change. Practices, behaviors, and attitudes that are not biblical exist in every culture. Missionaries must seek ways to introduce the new biblical patterns without overly disrupting the society. To immediately eliminate certain social practices may leave a void in the culture that would have serious consequences.

Such an elimination of cultural practices with serious consequences was experienced in a culture that demanded "bride price" in marriage relationships. Bride price called for a payment from the family of the groom to the family of the bride. Some Christians who came to work in the area thought this custom was buying the woman and forbade the Christians from practicing bride price. Marriages began to break up. The Christians then learned that bride price was a practice that gave stability to marriages. The families were involved in the marriage continuing. Taking bride price out of the society led to weakening marriages.

Some cultural practices must change if a society is to be biblical. A society that practiced human sacrifice would not continue this practice when the people came to conversion. A society that praised thievery and injustice would not continue these practices. The missionaries, however, will exercise extreme care in guiding the people to change in their cultural ways.

How will the missionaries guide to cultural change. The following steps will be helpful. First, seek to understand exactly what the place of the cultural practices holds in the society. What does this practice mean to the people? How does the practice function in the society?

With this understanding, the missionary must seek guidance from the Holy Spirit as to the procedure. Must this practice by eliminated? Must the practice be altered to have different meaning? Must the practice be continued with slight modification?

The missionary will then guide the people in the society to the biblical truth in regard to the practices. The missionary can be an advocate for change but never innovator, that is, the one who makes the change. This innovator must be a local leader, not an outsider. The missionary then will work with the local innovator.

The missionary will allow the local people to find the answers to the practice in the Scriptures. The local leaders may find help and guidance from the missionaries but the decisions will be their choice. Those changes that stem from the convictions of the local leaders are the changes that will become permanent and effective in the culture.

The missionaries will help the local leaders to find and implement what is called functional substitutes. Functional substitutes are new practices that are in line with biblical teachings that fill the cultural needs that the older practices filled. The concept that the husband must be a dominating, demanding leader is changed to the idea of a husband leading by the love of God and the example of Christ. The cultural need for a strong father is maintained while the more biblical model of servant leadership is introduced.

The process of leading to cultural change in the conversion experience is a delicate and demanding effort for missionaries and local Christian leaders. Short-term missionaries may not have time to participate fully in the process. They should, however, be aware of the necessities of such a process and not introduce factors that would make it more difficult.

The final goal of any cultural change is transformation of the society and culture to the will of God. Every society needs guidance toward this ultimate status. Every society falls short of God's will and every society needs to be guided toward biblical transformation. The process of introducing the gospel to a people is not complete until the society is transformed in the direction of God's ideal. Few tasks are more demanding than this effort.

The cultural adjustment must be reached in several areas:

- Cultural adjustment in the life style of the missionaries

- Cultural adjustment in the statement of the Gospel

- Cultural adjustment in the demands for salvation

- Cultural adjustment in the requirements of Christian living

- Cultural adjustment in the nature of the local church

- Cultural adjustment in the ways of worship in the churches

- Cultural adjustment in relation to the existing social structures and ideals

- Cultural adjustment in the selection of church leaders

Life Style Adjustments

No cultural adjustments are more important than those that relate to the life styles of the missionaries. Missionaries must follow biblical standards for behavior but also adjust to local customs of action. Ways of expressing respect vary from culture to culture and missionaries will respond in ways that are polite in the culture. Missionaries will adopt ways of eating, speaking, dressing, and relating that follow local customs so long as these customs do not conflict with biblical teachings.

One missionary expressed his plan in these words. He said, "In everything not sinful, Chinese." The more the missionary adjusts to local ways, the more effective will be his/her ministry among the people. Missionaries will never adopt any practice that is sinful or that threatens health. Missionaries will adopt every local practice that biblical teachings allow.

Exercises for This Section

1. In the following accounts, write what you think the missionaries should adopt as their ways of acting:

In a certain culture, the people never give or receive anything with the left hands.

In a certain culture, the people stand very close to others as they talk to them

In a certain culture, the women wear nothing above the waist

In a certain culture, the people eat with their fingers

In a certain culture, the people eat dog meat and consider it a delicacy

In a certain culture, the people seat persons who hold higher rank in the society in the best places

2.   Write some adjustments you would not make in trying to adjust to culture

_____

_____

_____

_____

_____

_____

Gospel Expression Adjustment

The biblical teachings cannot be changed but the ways of expressing biblical truth can be adjusted to cultures. In explaining biblical truth, missionaries should use local illustrations. They should explain biblical doctrine in local terms rather than using theological terms such as "regeneration." They should use local methods of communicating rather than leaning on Western ways.

Missionaries who desire to communicate the pure Gospel must find local ways to express these truths. They must use local means of speaking. They must use local languages and terminologies. They should refrain from using too many stories and accounts of their own countries. Good communication calls for explaining biblical truth in local terms.

Write your conclusions about the following expressions of biblical teachings.

Exercises for This Section

1. Bread was the staple of diet in Jesus' day. Rice is the staple of diet in much of the world today. What about the person who teaches that Jesus is the Rice of Life?

_____

_____

_____

_____

_____

2. The missionary states that Jesus will justify the one who believes. What problem in communication might this missionary face?

_____
_____
_____
_____
_____
_____

3. Pointing at another is a sign of disrespect but the missionary who was trained in Western preaching, uses pointing to emphasize his message

_____
_____
_____
_____

Demands for Salvation Adjustments

Salvation involves change. One changes from a sinner to one in the Kingdom of God—to a child of God. This conversion demands certain changes. But what are the necessary changes? These necessary changes may vary from culture to culture.

What in one culture must be changed may not exist in another culture. One culture may involve allowing open sexual experience among teen aged people and another may not. The change needed in the first culture is not needed in the second.

The procedure in introducing change follows these steps:

- Ask the Holy Spirit to reveal those practices and ideas that need to be changed

- Make certain the practices and ideals that the missionary thinks need changing are based on biblical teachings and not on the missionary's cultural background

- Guide the people to discover the need for the changes

- Allow the people to create the changes

- Lead the people to introduce the changes

- Project the goal of transformation

Christian Living Adjustments

Missionaries have called for adjustments in life style for new converts that are more cultural than biblical. Some missionaries have insisted that converts stop smoking and attending movies. While smoking is obviously harmful to health and all would be better off without the practice, one can be a Christian and still smoke. Movies often present unbiblical conduct and attitudes but are not directly forbidden to believers. Working in sinful businesses (such as casinos) is not a good environment for Christians but Christians may not be required to immediately give up their jobs when they come to Christ.

Adjustments to living will be a part of the Christian experience. The adjustments and changes may take the form of a process. Those changes demanded by biblical teachings (stealing, adultery, injustice, trickery, gossip, slander, etc) should be put out of the Christian life and those fruits of love, peace, integrity, kindness, gentleness, care for others, etc. become part of the believer's life. The change most often does not come immediately but over a period of growth. The missionary must allow this period of growth as people, like societies, are transformed.

Local Church Adjustments

Local churches should fit the receiving societies and cultures and not be patterned after the practices of the sending culture. I once worshipped with a Christian group in a tropical environment. The pastors in the group wore long black robes with lace at the collars and sleeves. The dress was totally out of line with the culture. Long black robes and lace are not suited for the tropics.

Why did the pastors dress as they did? They did so because the missionaries who came hundreds of years before dressed that way because it was the proper attire for pastors in the sending culture. The local church should follow the ways of the local culture and not be copied from some foreign patterns. Local patterns, so long as in line with biblical principles, should be encouraged in the local churches.

Ways of Worship Adjustments

In every society, music, behavior, and practices differ as people engage in rituals and social activities. Missionaries do not insist that the people adopt the exact ways of worship that are followed in the missionaries' culture. Times of worship, the types of music, the means of proclaiming the message, and other factors in worship should be local and not brought in from the sending culture.

Many Christian groups in the United States have found that younger people respond to different types of music and other practices than have been traditional in the churches. The churches that have been effective in reaching these younger people have adopted the new music and methods. Missionaries should allow worship services to be adapted to the local society. The goal is not to present the worship in the ways of the sending group but in the means most acceptable by the receiving group so long as no biblical principles are compromised.

Church Leaders Adjustments

People from the West have become accustomed to leaders who are highly trained and certified by the denominations of groups with which they serve. Such leaders may not be available in the regions the missionaries serve. Untrained and unordained leaders may be the only leaders available.

Missionaries may need to accept the possibility of untrained leaders and leaders who are not ordained to guide the churches and Christians in area of their missionary work. These leaders should be free to provide the leadership that is needed—including preaching, baptizing, leading the Lord's Supper, marrying, and burying.

Training of leaders for the churches is obviously a most needed and significant ministry. The problem has been, however, that leadership training has focused on training the full-time, fully trained, career leaders. The greatest leadership need is for lay leaders who can start and lead the many small groups of believers. The acceptance of the places of lay leaders is critical for the continuing expansion of Christianity.

Exercises for This Section

1.   Your leader will read you some accounts of cultural situations in relation to missionary service. Write below your responses as to activities and attitudes that must be changed (If you have no leader, secure the PowerPoint Presentation that goes with this booklet and read the accounts in the notes section of the appropriate cells)

_____
_____
_____
_____
_____
_____
_____
_____
_____
_____

2.   Your leader will read some accounts of changes introduced into cultures. Indicate your position on these introductions to change. (If you have no leader, secure the PowerPoint Presentation that goes with this booklet and read the accounts in the notes section of the appropriate cells)

_____
_____
_____
_____
_____
_____
_____
_____

Training in Safety Measures

As a missionary going into a different culture either in another nation or a different section of your own country, you may be subject to danger. Some dangers stem from health factors and others from realities in the target country or area. Missionaries are wise to consider and practice protective measures wherever they serve.

Eating and drinking in other cultures can threaten the missionaries' health. This threat stems not only from unsanitary conditions in the new culture but simply from the fact that different germs are present in different places. People coming to America from other lands often face certain health risks due to the different set of bacteria they encounter.

Missionaries should seek advice from others who have been in the areas to be served as to eating and drinking practices. Other health factors should be considered. A sick missionary is seldom an effective missionary. Missionaries should seek to protect their health but also accept the possibility of sickness.

The areas to which missionaries go are not always more dangerous in terms of physical safety than the missionaries' own country. In visiting another region, however, missionaries are wise to ask about dangers and threats to safety. Simple avoidance of danger and dangerous areas can allow for more effective service.

Missionaries should seek out advice on immunizations that are wise for the regions they expect to serve. To forego immunizations shows no greater faith in God. God provides the immunizations. Missionaries should seek training in protective measures and follow the best advice they can get for living in the new surroundings.

Training in Ways of Witnessing

Christians can choose from and use many acceptable and effective methods for witnessing. So long as these methods do not conflict with biblical teachings are open for witnesses. Your particular training for your short-term mission experience will provide training in the methods that your group will use. Here we will mention only some general guidelines for witnessing, especially to people in cultures different from our own.

Adhering to general guidelines

- Show respect for the culture and religion of the people to whom you are witnessing

- Use communication techniques that are understandable and acceptable for the people in the receptor culture

- Use language that is most expressive for the people in the receiving culture

- Explain Christian teachings in terms easily understood by the people in the receiving culture. Avoid theological terms that have little meaning to the unsaved and unchurched

- Move the people toward a positive decision to accept Christ as Savior. Seek the Spirit's leadership in knowing when to ask the receiving person for a decision

- Promise the people only what the Bible promises, that is, Eternal Life in Christ. Stay away from any "health and wealth" expression of Christianity

- Leave the door open to return to share the Good News in an other witnessing experience

Exercises for This Section

1. Write some difficult to understand theological terms Christians sometimes use in witnessing. How would you explain these terms in easily understood terms.

_____

_____

_____

_____

_____

_____

_____

_____

_____

_____

_____

2. What biblical truths do you think should be a part of your witness to the unsaved or unchurched person?

_____

_____

_____

_____

_____

_____

_____

_____

_____

3. What is wrong with the "health and wealth" teachings in regard to salvation?

_____

_____

_____

_____

_____

_____

_____

_____

4. Write some culturally inappropriate teachings that one might fall into using

_____

_____

_____

_____

_____

_____

_____

_____

_____

Using your own testimony in the witnessing situation

One of the most effective means of sharing the Good News with the lost and unchurched is your own testimony. You would do well to write your testimony and study the way your express it in the witnessing situation. Tell the person how you became a follower of Jesus Christ.

Exercises for This Section

1. Write your testimony of salvation. Ask others to help you make it more easily understood

_____
_____
_____
_____
_____
_____
_____
_____
_____
_____
_____
_____

2. Anticipate some problems in the witnessing situation. Write some answers to questions you expect to face.

_____
_____
_____
_____
_____
_____

Developing Ministry Skills

You are a missionary and as a missionary you have gifts or skills you can use in missionary work. You probably have skills and gifts beyond your present realizations. That is to say, you can most likely do far more missionary service than you dream you can do. To become fully the missionary you are, you should strive to develop your ministry skills.

The process of developing ministry skills is to recognize and discover your spiritual gifts. Every Christian has spiritual gifts. Spiritual gifts are abilities to use talents for the glory of God and service of man. Talents become spiritual gifts when the Spirit of God unlocks the talent to be effective in God's service.

No Christian has all the spiritual gifts and no spiritual gift is intended for all Christians (except the gift of love). The Bible mentions spiritual gifts (Rom 12:3-8; 1 Cor 12:1-11) but I am convinced the Bible does not mention every ability that can be used for God's glory and service. You have gifts. Find out what your gifts are and allow God to use them.

Once the Christian accepts that he/she has gifts that God can use in His worldwide plan of redemption, that believer should seek to develop and refine the gift. The developing and refining of the gifts depends on God's power just as the initial giving of gift is through the Spirit.

Christians can find development for their gifts by training. While training is important, an even better way to develop the spiritual gifts comes through using them in God's service. The Holy Spirit who gives the gifts, also empowers the believer to use them.

Some Christians have a gift for communicating spiritual truth. If this ability is your gift, train to communicate better but also begin to communicate to others the great message of Jesus Christ. Some Christians have the gift of comforting. If this is your gift, use it for His glory and the service of humankind while you study and train to increase your effectiveness as a comforter.

These messages could continue to mention every spiritual gift. The idea is to discover the gifts God has given you, begin to use them in His service, and as you do, train to increase your effectiveness in the use of the gift. Do not wait to serve until you are fully trained. The Spirit will use you in His service as you commit your gift to Him.

Do not turn from an opportunity because you feel you are not gifted in that service. God can use you. You might even find through the effort a gift you were not aware you have. If a service is needed, learn as much as you can about how to fulfill the need.

As you begin the life as a missionary, a missional Christian, seek ways to develop as many ministry skills as you can. In this effort you will find some skills that indicate that you are gifted in that area. You can serve most effectively in the areas in which you are spiritually gifted. You can, however, in His power, serve effectively even in areas for which you are not directly gifted.

Whatever is needed for a church's ministry will be provided through the Spirit. Train and develop your abilities and skills so as to be available to the Spirit. God will work through you and your preparation.

You may be called upon to perform some ministry for which you do not feel gifted and for which you have not received training. Do not fear. The Holy Spirit can make use of all you say and do in His power.

You are a missionary. As you go, wherever you go, serve Him, make disciples, guide believers, care for people, proclaim the Message of Jesus Christ.

Bringing the person to the salvation experience

Bringing the person to the actual experience of accepting Christ is not always an easy task. Knowing the eternal significance of the person's conversion to Jesus, however, leads to boldness on the witnesses' part. Do not be hesitant to ask the person to express an acceptance of Jesus. Do not be caught in the dilemma of fearing that the person does not understand enough.

The Holy Spirit can overcome all lack of knowledge. Trust the Spirit to make clear the message. Be as through as you can be in presenting the Message and trust the person's understanding to the Spirit. You have every right to ask for a decision. Eternity hangs in the balance. A part of the witnessing experience is that of asking the person to accept Jesus.

Exercises for This Section

1. Suggest ways in which you might introduce a witness to Christ into your dealing with a person.

_____

_____

_____

_____

_____

_____

_____

_____

2. Why can you have assurance and confidence as you witness to a lost person?

_____

_____

_____

_____

_____

_____

_____

_____

Training in Means of Serving

A vital part of missional living for Christians and churches is that of serving the people by meeting their spiritual and physical needs. As missionaries of Jesus Christ, we are called on to render both spiritual and material aid to the people. Often the process of meeting physical needs opens the minds and hearts of the people to receive the spiritual witness of salvation in Christ.

As missionaries we do not, however, do our ministry to physical needs simply to open doors for witness. We serve people because it is the nature of redeemed people and redeemed groups to serve in every way. The relief of suffering and the filling of needs are spiritual ministries.

Missionaries need, therefore, to train in means of serving the physical needs of the people to whom they minister. The exact training will be tailored to the precise needs of the people to be served. Missionaries, especially short-term servants, would do well to find out what the needs are and seek some training in meeting these needs.

Missionaries should observe several general guidelines as they prepare for and provide services to the people. These guidelines include:

- Seek detailed understanding of the needs and how these needs can be met

- Accept the fact that some needs may be beyond the technical ability of your group

- Seek trained persons to accompany if special needs challenge the training and knowledge of the people going on the ministry

- Seek training in the areas of need with the understanding that some ministries may not be open to you

- Accept the fact that providing funds that go far beyond the abilities of the receiving group may not relieve the situation. Money may not be the total answer

- Perform the ministries as an expression of the love of Christ and not out of desire for admiration, fame, or praise

- Allow witnessing possibilities to come out of the ministries and respond to the possibilities

- Remember that all you do has the goal of bringing praise and glory to God

Exercises for This Section

1. Write the needs of the people to whom you are going.

_____
_____
_____
_____
_____
_____
_____
_____
_____
_____

2. List the skills and knowledge that your group will need to meet these needs

_____
_____
_____
_____
_____
_____
_____
_____
_____
_____

3. List some matters you think your group should guard against in providing physical aid during the ministry

_____

Session 4

Missional Christians and Churches: Where and When?

Too often, Christians see mission beginning when they arrive at some other place. They envision a time and place where their mission will begin. Many times, Christians are in training for a mission trip and they look forward to beginning their "mission" when that time comes and they arrive at that place.

These thoughts are understandable and acceptable so long as they do not blind the believers to the tremendous possibilities of mission right where they are. Too many Christians become overly excited about missionary activities in the other place and fail to practice any missionary efforts at home. One man often went on "mission trips" and came back with testimonies of witnessing and victories. This same man, however, seldom if ever, participated in visiting the lost and needy in his own community. *Where and when for missional Christians means right here and right now.*

Recent events in the world have brought many different peoples to the United States. One can experience many opportunities to witness to people of other cultures right here in the United States. Multitudes of needy people exist in every community. Believers have unlimited possibilities of Christian service to many people in their own communities. The statement that mission fields have come to America is certainly an accurate observation. Missional Christians and churches make full use of this opportunity.

Short-Term Missions Today

Mission trips are good opportunities for missional Christians and Churches. These same types of opportunities exist in the communities of the believers and their churches. Missional living and service is available in every place and every time. The "When and Where" for missional living and service is here and now.

Missional Christians and missional Churches should study their neighborhoods to find groups of people who need the ministry of the Lord. Lost people are around us on every side. Needy people cry out for someone to express the love of God to them. We must never become so concerned about the spiritually needy people in other lands and places that we overlook the spiritually needy in our own communities.

Exercises for this Section

1. Write below the spiritual needs you understand exist in the people you are going to serve on a mission trip.

_____

_____

_____

_____

_____

_____

_____

_____

_____

_____

_____

2.   Seek to discover groups of people in your own neighborhoods that have many of the same needs. Write a description of these people below.

_____
_____
_____
_____
_____
_____
_____
_____
_____

3.   Formulate plans for reaching the spiritually needy in the place intended for your mission trip.

_____
_____
_____
_____
_____
_____
_____
_____

4.   Formulate plans for reaching the spiritually needy in your own neighborhood

_____
_____
_____
_____

_____
_____
_____
_____
_____

5.   Write your understanding of the fact that both the
       people in the area of the mission trip and those in
       your own neighborhood are people who need the
       Lord.

_____
_____
_____
_____
_____
_____
_____
_____
_____

Doing Missions Today

The when for missionary work is now. Waiting for the
right time to begin to function as a missional Christian and
a missional church is a loosing situation. Christians may
look forward to the opportunities for missional service when
the time for a mission trip arises. Christians should also,
seek out opportunities for these missional activities at the
present time and in the present situation.

The Christian who does not express missional character in his/her own situation will likely not be an effective
witness in the "mission field." The world is the field and
missional Christians should see missional opportunities on

every side. Every community provides extensive openings for missional service.

Exercises for This Section

1. Write your commitment to the ministry to which your group is directed.

_____

_____

_____

_____

_____

_____

_____

2. Indicate some skills and practices you need to gain as you prepare for these ministries.

_____

_____

_____

_____

_____

_____

Session 5

Christian Commitment to Missional Living

Missional Christian living, missional church life, and missional church ministries do not just happen. Believers become missional Christians and churches become missional churches only by serious effort and the indispensable empowering of God's Holy Spirit. The process of becoming a missional Christian and a missional church demands a commitment to allow the Holy Spirit to empower us for such living and serving.

The experience of salvation provides all a person needs to become a missional Christian. God promises that the divine power of God gives us everything we need for life and godliness.

> ³His divine power has given us everything we need for life and godliness through our knowledge of him who called us by his own glory and goodness. ⁴Through these he has given us his very great and precious promises, so that through them you may participate in the divine nature and escape the corruption in the world caused by evil desires (2 Peter 1:3-4 NIV).

All any believer needs for Christians living and Christian service is available through God's power.

With this tremendous potential at our finger tips, we all too often fail to allow the power to flow and the Christian life and service to thrive. Salvation is ever available to any who call on the Name of the Lord:

> For God so loved the world that he gave his one and only Son, that whoever believes in him shall not perish but have eternal life. ¹⁷For God did not send his Son into the world to condemn

the world, but to save the world through him. [18]Whoever believes in him is not condemned, but whoever does not believe stands condemned already because he has not believed in the name of God's one and only Son. [19]This is the verdict: Light has come into the world, but men loved darkness instead of light because their deeds were evil. [20]Everyone who does evil hates the light, and will not come into the light for fear that his deeds will be exposed. [21]But whoever lives by the truth comes into the light, so that it may be seen plainly that what he has done has been done through God."

[36]**Whoever believes in the Son has eternal life**, but whoever rejects the Son will not see life, for God's wrath remains on him" (John 3:16-21, 36 NIV).

[12]For there is no difference between Jew and Gentile—the same Lord is Lord of all and richly blesses all who call on him, [13]for, "**Everyone who calls on the name of the Lord will be saved**" (Rom 10:12-13 NIV).

Many, in spite of this gracious offer, never reach out to Jesus Christ and remain in their sins. Availability does not always translate to actually receiving.

The same reality exists in relation to missional living and missional churches. The power to become a missional Christian and a missional church is ever available. Too many fail to avail themselves of this power and consequently never reach the level of missional Christian living. Many churches remain embedded in self-centered ways of living and never become missional churches.

Christians, who fail to reach the level of missional living, sacrifice the ultimate joys of Christian life. Churches, that fail to reach the level of missional congregations, remain of limited service when unbounded effectiveness is readily available. The tragedy exists for the Christians, the churches, and for all those who could be served by these Christians and churches.

God does not force people to become His followers. Salvation does not come by coercion. Eternal life comes to those who reach out in faith to the gracious offer of God. Response is necessary.

Missional Christian living does not happen apart from the willingness of the believer to allow God to empower and equip him/her for this kind of living. The living of the missional Christians comes by grace as much as the salvation of the believer comes by grace. As God does not overpower the sinner and force him/her to come to faith, the Lord will not force any one of us to become a missional Christian. He will not force any congregation to become missional.

In each case, the believer and the congregation can commit to becoming missional. The way to missional level is a process but it is a process that must willingly joined. Missional living, on the individual and the congregational level, demands commitment.

Will you commit to allowing God through the Holy Spirit to transform you into a missional Christian? Will you commit to helping your church, also by God's empowering Spirit, become a missional church? If you and your church are already on this journey, will you commit to continuing in this path?

This small book has the purpose of encouraging every believer in every congregation to begin or continue the process to becoming totally missional. It seeks to stimulate believers and churches to turn from self-serving, self-seeking ways to service. It urges believers and churches to actually do missions and become missionary. It seeks to guide believers and churches to move beyond being mission-minded to becoming mission centered.

You are a missionary. You can become an even more effective missionary. Your church is a missionary body. It can become a more effective mission body as it moves along the process of becoming a missional church. Our responsibilities as believers and churches are to move in the direction of missional living and service.

The Subtitle to this book is: *A Guide for Believers Who Desire to Become Missional Christians in Missional Churches.* May God grant you the grace to commit to His plan for you to become a missional Christian in a missional church.

My Commitment to Seek to Become a Missional Christian

My Commitment to help my church become a missional church